Creating your Journey

by

Patricia

Copyright © 1999 by
Patricia A Hanrahan
First Printing 1999

All rights reserved. No part of this publication may be reproduced or transmitted in any form or by any means, electronic or mechanical, including photocopy, without permission in writing from A Balance and Harmony, at the address below.

A Balance and Harmony
PO Box 67058
Topeka, Kansas 66667-0058
Phone (785) 272-2415
E-Mail address: patricia@balanceandharmony.com
Web site address: WWW.balanceandharmony.com

ISBN: 0-9671406-0-9

Printed in the United States of America

Cover Rose Design:————-Phyllis Hunter
Typeset Design & Graphics:—Steve Hanrahan

Author is available for workshops to assist you in creating your personal journey.

Table of Contents

PREFACE	vii
ACKNOWLEDGMENTS	ix
INTRODUCTIONS	xi
1. CREATING THE JOURNEY OF LIFE	1
A. CONNECTING TO THE UNIVERSE	5
B. AFFIRMATIONS	9
C. CHAKRAS	15
D. MEDITATIONS	21
E. VISUALIZATIONS	31
F. GOALS AND JOURNALS	43
2. CONNECTION WITH UNIVERSAL SPIRITS	47
A. GIVING	49
B. WORKING IN SILENCE	53
C. GIVE OUT BLESSINGS	55
D. PROTECTION FOR YOURSELF AND OTHERS	57
E. SPECIAL UNIVERSAL BLESSINGS	59
3. MAGICAL SOLUTIONS	63
A. GET YOUR PARKING PLACE	65
B. FINDING LOST ARTICLES	67
C. CREATING YOUR COUNCIL	73
D. CREATING YOUR NEW POSITION IN LIFE	77
E. WORKING WITH ILLNESS	79
F. WORKING WITH YOUR HIGHER POWER	81
G. WORKING WITH OTHERS	85
H. CLEANING OUT YOUR SPACE	87
4. THE BLESSING	91
5. GLOSSARY	93

To the reader,

    This book is the answer to *my truth*. It is information given to me for my understanding of the purpose of life and the spiritual path to find the connection back to the light of the divine. The purpose of this book is to open doors to enhance your life journey.

    There is a glossary in the back of this book to help you with unfamiliar words.

The rose on the cover of this book is a symbol of love, it was painted by Phyllis Hunter, my dear friend since childhood, as an expression of love. Red roses, to me always symbolize love, and it is my desire is to share with you the essence of love that went into this book. This book is based on many sources including following.

- From my research
- From attending seminars and reading books
- Through my Guardian Angel from the heavens Gabriel (Gabriel is the head of the heavenly guards and the Prince of Justice)
- Through the other angels who connect with me including Michael and Rafael. (Michael is the chief archangel. Rafael is in charge of healing)
- Through my dear best friends and earth angels Karla Worley, Geni Mofid, Wayne Kelpin, Susan Shelby, and Judy Walton.
- Through my children, a part of my creation who are so special to me, Kari, Steve, Craig, and Shane. Also my grandchildren Tanner and Amber and, to my mother, Pearl.

- And through all who have assisted me in so many acts of love leading to the creation of this book.

Red roses to all of you who choose to read this expression of my love.
Create your life with red roses and love.

INTRODUCTION

In my soul, I knew there were answers to my curious mind. I wanted to understand the creative forces of the universe. After years of reading, meditation, and quietness on my part, a certain understanding began to unfold. It is this understanding I seek to share with you through this book.

I was told the world began with absolute silence. Out of that silence came an energy source. Out of that energy is light, out of light came sound. Out of the light and sound is the original creation of all that is. The energy manifested itself into a vibrant frequency. Everything that exists is a range of energy frequencies, each with its own purpose. There are higher and lower vibrations. The rock may be a lower vibration than the tree, the tree lower than the animal. Humans are a high vibration. One form of energy however, is not more important than another. All are a God source of divine energy, the positive form of unconditional love.

The soul begins its travel with 1000 other souls. We group with the band of souls as life travel companions, supporting each other through the journey.

Together, and as individuals, we experience lessons that serve to both design and fulfill our purpose in life. Dharma defines the natural and moral principles and order that apply to everything in existence. It is your purpose in life. What are you doing to make yourself and those around you happy? Are you living with good intentions? Are you working together with those around you to achieve love, harmony, and happiness? You should love yourself and serve others in the way you want to be served.

We must understand the role of the ego. The ego is the self. It is the actual motive of all conscious action. Many times, the ego stands in our way. The ego can limit our outlook and we become self-centered. When you find your goals and live your lessons without fear, judgment, and control, let the ego go, you will find your Dharma, the ultimate harmony and happiness.

Achieving these life goals, traveling this journey is meant to be a joint effort, working with others along the way. Together, we decide what lessons are to be learned, get with our groups and design a family. Each member knows the part he or she will play to assist the other in the plan. Each individual will create a crisis to assist him or her to awaken the soul. Every soul is monitored. Once we come to Earth, we forget what was known in any former existence we may have had and what we have assigned ourselves as a lesson. If you remembered all, how would you accomplish the lessons you are here to learn?

Lessons are learned through the people around us and through experiences that come our way. Sometimes we call these experiences coincidences, events, or happenings that appear to be arranged to indicate coincidence or coexistence. These events are synchronized and appear to occur when we need them the most. All the events of life are there because at some level we drew them to ourselves. If you can be prepared to give up all your preconceived notions and go with the plan, the design for your life, you will find synchronization is planned by you and your universe for your best being. Actually, there are no coincidences in your plan. Everything will appear to you at the right time and place as part of your life lessons.

We have been given the responsibility of thought. Each thought ripples throughout the universe. Every thought, word, and deed is recorded in our own Akashic records. The Akashic record is like a computer record of all your souls' travels since its beginning. This record contains all the forms of Karma accrued on your path. In addition to your family, you are given spiritual teachers to guide you. These teachers are ascended masters, guardian angels, and others of the spiritual world. We strive to experience meaningful lessons to raise our higher consciousness. The goal is to stay in the power of light and love, to stay in balance and harmony with the universe and to return to God's pure *love.*

My friend Sam had a 90 year old lady who worked for him as a housekeeper. While she worked, this lady constantly mumbled "undefoube and obeefoube, undefoube and obeefoube." Sam asked me what the words meant to me. I thought about it for awhile and finally decided they express a higher energy and a lower energy. When Sam asked the lady what they meant, she replied, "What comes around, goes around." This made me think about all the levels of energy and how we treat them. What we give out should be what we want to receive. When you water plants, they reward you with flowers. When you feed your dog, he looks at you as his master. Every kind action brings about rewards and good Kharma.

My understanding is that once the assigned lessons are learned, the soul leaves for higher worlds. Your soul will leave earth, but will not resume new lessons until joined by others in the group of souls. This is one reason for the importance of assisting every soul you are in contact with. We advance when we learn to act responsibly. The departure from this existence is not to be feared. It is a process of exiting the physical body. When this happens, you may hover around a while, then you will move into a tunnel. Some spirit will meet you with light of unconditional love. You will arrive at a place of healing, and at that point, you will do a review of your life and your self-judgment. You will access your Akashic records. You will connect with your soul family. In this place of tranquillity and peace, you begin to regroup and decide what is needed for future spiritual development.

Again the lesson for earth is to learn *love and*

light. When we learn to forgive and give unconditional love, we are there. We acknowledge our purpose and become closer to the God source.

Welcome to the world of Balance and Harmony.

Creating the journey of life

You are reading this because it was always intended for this moment. You are about to embark upon a journey. This may be new information or connect with things you already know. This information is given to assist you in your adventure of this life. This is not intended to interfere with your belief system. This will enhance your life.

The steps to follow on this journey are connecting with the universe, meditation, affirmations, and visualizations. We meditate to get ourselves in connection with the universe. We do affirmations to confirm our belief and desires. We state our intentions to extend to ourselves and others a positive creation, and we connect with the souls around us and our angels.

We can start by changing the pattern of our lives. Three ways to do this is through meditation, affirmations, and visualizations on a daily basis. Once you get into this mode, you will begin to see life unfolding in a new way. It is helpful to ask who some of the angels are that are around you. They have names. Ask them for their name, but do not be surprised if it is unusual. It becomes more personal to know the name of your very special angel. Know there are many to serve you, but one is the special guardian angel for you.

One day my grandson, Tanner, was telling me the TV wasn't working. I didn't have a clue how to fix it. I was working on it and not getting any results, so I asked my guardian angel Gabriel to help me. The TV magically came on. My grandson asked me, "Who is this Gabriel who fixes the TV?" I told him, "He is my Guardian Angel. " The next day Tanner asked me if he had a Guardian Angel. I told him "Yes. " He wanted to know his name. I told him I didn't know. I told him to be really quiet some time and ask, "What is my Guardian Angel's name?" Tanner later told me he received his answer. His angel is Raphael. He also told me the TV was acting up again and he told me he asked Gabriel and Raphael to come over and fix the TV. He said it worked. We had a discussion about the TV being old and only so much angel power could be expected! We have some work to do on angel assistance.

Now, let us begin by a review of the basics needed to start you on your way.

In this book, you will find places where the information has been repeated. This is because information is more easily retained when read more than once. After some of the chapters, there will be exercises for you to use to start this process of assisting you in your life journey.

Connecting to the Universe

Angels: a spiritual being superior to man in power and intelligence.

𝒯here are angels among us. Some people prefer to call them guides or spirits. They are our connection to the One/God. They are here to assist, guide, and protect us. They have not been awarded a human body, so they can always be with us. The Angelic Kingdom is a grand embodiment of maternal love, embracing all of humanity in its caring, nurturing wings, a glorious gift provided for us. Many people are suffering heartaches and need to connect, to create uplifting changes. Most of the time, people call on angels in times of crisis, looking for a miracle. These messengers from God are available to use their energies on upon request. There are times when we need a power greater than we believe we have. Angels appear in many forms. Think of the times when you have felt their presence.

Many people acknowledge the presence of angels when they are on top of a mountain. Some feel them when they are near water, a stream, or the ocean. You feel them when for no reason; a breeze gently comes by or a sweet aroma floats in. There are times when you shiver for no reason. Angels let you know they are available.

They are pure love and know no boundaries. Connect with them. You can communicate silently or verbally. They wish to be your companions. They will never leave you or deceive you.

Everyone has one special angel called the Guardian Angel. Ask for yours by name. It feels more personal when you know who they are. They are always there but must have permission to reach out a hand to the one who calls.

When there is a request for help, the angels will be quicker and more powerful to answer the call. Sometimes the answer to the request or assistance may not be what you expect or desire. But remember the answer will be in your highest interest. We all have lessons in life. What is presented to us via our experiences is to assist in our life's life path. The angels stand ready to assist in all ways. They understand your sorrow, pain, and confusion. They can soften and lift burdens from your shoulders. There is a Celestial Hierarchy. Celestial refers to a heavenly or mythical being. There are levels of hierarchy among angels. The highest are the archangels Michael, Gabriel, Raphael, and Uriel. There are three angel groups. First are the angels, and archangels. Second are the principles, powers, virtues, dominions, and thrones. The third are the cherubim, and seraphim. Each has particular tasks. For example, thrones administer justice and powers keep order. There are teams of angels. You can request to assist you. The Angel Realm is a part of your present to function as energetic facilitators, to boost and invigorate your choices. Allow this team to help you resolve and focus on your unity with all creation and the Oneness of God. The reality is Oneness. Humans have created the experience of separateness from the God energy as an enrichment exercise on earth. The overall goal of this experience is to bring more light to the creation of each moment, as you shift from duality to Oneness, becoming closer to God.

Affirmations

*A*ffirmations are statements made in the form of a *positive* assertion. Affirmations are made to confirm our beliefs in what we desire our life to be. It is helpful to set in motion a list of what you desire. When we state our intentions they become our reality. It has a mirroring effect that what we state is what we get. We always give our lists or statements in a way that affirms it has already happened. We assume it is so. It is good to sit down and take time to write your affirmations out on paper. Write everything you want in this life. Be very careful in your requests and be sure it is what you desire. If you requested a million dollars, are you willing to pay any price to get it? For instance what if you had to be in a car accident and sued another person to get the money. Would that be worth it? Consider what is really important to you in your journey. What would really make your life as good as it can be? You will see the changes. Make sure it is always for the good of your higher self. Your affirmations can be toward lifestyles, health, employment, relationships, environment, finances or anything else you choose. You can always add to or change this list. Try to remember them at least once a day.

Be humble. Be patient. *Do not try to be big. Be small*, until you almost become a nothing, which is better for you than being a large thing in the world, a cynosure of all eyes. Be confident that you will get what you need.

Always remember these three things.

1. Be *clear* as to what you want.
2. Be sure that *you will get* what you want.
3. Start with that effort *now*.

You will succeed always, and with everything.

You could make three columns.

In the first write, "What do you want?"(What are you in search of?)

In the second column, "Can you achieve it?"(Take analysis of your own capacities in the search of your wants.)

In the third column, "What is the way to it?" (This is the practical aspect of your search.)

After you complete these columns, begin your

list of affirmations. Knowing this will align you up to all your needs to completeness.

We do things and ask because we have an aim or purpose. We are in search of it and work for its fulfillment.

A list might start like this:
1. I am a being of light and love.
2. Abundance comes to me easily.
3. I deserve all that I have and I am grateful.
4. Everything in my life comes perfectly and effortlessly.
5. I accept that my life has perfect health.
6. My life is full of opportunities.
7. I have created a life of fun, great family, and friends.
8. I have harmony and peace in my life.

You always thank your God, Higher Power, Angels and /or Spirits for their assistance.

Affirmations

We do things and ask because we have an aim or purpose. We are in search of it and work for its fulfillment.

Always remember three things.
1. Be clear *as to what you want.*
2. *Be sure that you will get* what you want. Do not be hesitant.
3. Start with that effort *now.* Do not say *tomorrow.*

You will succeed always, and with everything.

Complete the following information.

What do you want? (What are you in search for?)

You can achieve it by? (Take analysis of your own capacities in the search of your wants.)

What is the way to it? (This is the practical aspect of your search.)

Begin writing your list of affirmations.

Chakras

The chakras comes from the teachings of Abraham. In the Egyptian era, they used it to work to connect to the God force. In the Western world, some of us have not understood the chakras and how to use this information. The eastern cultures have been aware of the chakras and use them in meditation and healing. There are seven main chakras in the human body. The following information is the location in the body and the color associated with each chakra. First is the root (located at the lumbar area) and red. Second is the navel and orange. Third is the solar plexus and yellow. Fourth is the heart and green. Fifth is the throat and blue. Sixth is the third eye and violet. Seventh is the crown and white. Each chakra relates to that part of the body. The chakras are connected to us spiritually. Chakras have an energy that runs up and down the spine. This energy begins at the base of the spine and spirals upward to the head. As we evolve doing meditation each of these chakras opens more fully, supporting our transformation of higher powers. When the chakras are rotating smoothly, the body is in balance. The primary function of the chakra is to keep the life force energy flowing smoothly. Individuals and healers work with the chakras to provide a balance among our emotions, our will, and our reason. Blockage in the paths of the chakras leads to body breakdown and disease.

The kundalini is a source of power located at the base of the spine. It is like an electrical fluid that moves along the center of the body and through the major chakras. Sometimes kundalini releases itself when a person is in deep meditation. When this power is released it develops a new awareness and to aid spiritual growth.

There are therapists and others who know how to go in and reset your chakras, and help you balance by taking the universal light in our right hand, and providing it to your chakras with the left hand.

We can connect our energy path by connecting our electrical path by using polority therapy. There is a breakdown in one of your systems when the electrical path is broken. This can help you temporarily, but you have to do the work. You must connect and clear out all negative energy. When you meditate, you are aligning the body with the spiritual energy of the higher/God/world. You find the chakras get involved because they are connected to the spirit and soul, as well as the physical body. It is important to have an understanding of their purpose.

Chakra Chart

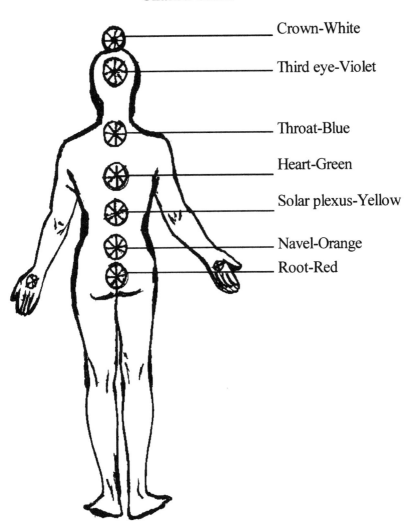

Meditations

Centering your soul

*M*editation allows one to focus one's thoughts to plan or project the mind. If you meditate on a regular basis, you will find that you are more centered and balanced. There are many ways of meditating. This practice can lead your life lessons. This is also a way of releasing stress. Many people find they have less pain and are calmer when using meditation.

Here is one you may want to try:

To begin, sit on the floor with your legs crossed and your arms extended up toward the heavens or have your hands placed on your legs with your palms upward. Your hands receive the light and energy. You will feel the light; you may shiver or feel a tingling as it comes in. Be aware of your breathing. Follow the breath in and out. Try to eliminate all chatter that comes to mind. When outside noises come in, move your mind back to the quietness.

Find the stillness. After a few sessions it becomes easier to shut out noise. You will be able to sit longer. The amount of time can be increased as you go along. The meditation should allow you to feel relaxed and closer to your higher self and your higher power. It makes it easy to cope with life and feel peace. Some people like to have a candle burning during meditation.

 This is another form of meditation:

Find yourself a quiet place. Shut your eyes. Take a few deep breaths. Now as you exhale, let go of the tensions of the day. You may need to shake a few muscles loose if they are tight. As you inhale, feel your energy gather into a tight ball, allowing you to become more self-contained with each in breath. With each out breath, let yourself release tensions. Do this several times.

Your consciousness, your awareness has been scattered. Your mind is here and there. With each in breath, draw your consciousness back to you. It may take some time to release the chatter that comes to you. The more you practice, the more you are able to shut out the chatter.

As you breathe, feel your energy becoming more dense and contained. Feel it circulating within and around your body. Relax and feel your own self gathered in, becoming more resonant with each breath. Each time you find your mind reaching out to other things, gently bring it back and invite it to be in your body.

Now, imagine you are on a beach near the ocean in Hawaii. You are laying on the beach, on the warm white sand. Imagine, as you lay there, the sun is shining down and warming you. Feel the warm, hot sand as you sink deeper into it. You are so relaxed, calm, and quiet. Your body is getting so warm. You feel the sun all over you. It is so hot. Now, look to the side and see the ocean. The waves are coming in and going out, coming in and going out. It is so peaceful, so quiet. Smell the ocean. See it as blue, clear, beautiful water. Look up and see the beautiful blue sky and the white clouds floating around. Look at the birds gently floating around the clouds. What a lovely sunny day.

Think about your feet and how they are so relaxed. Tell them to be quiet and relaxed. Tell your calves to be quiet and relaxed, and feel them sinking into the hot sand. Talk to your upper legs and hips. Tell them to be quiet, calm, and relaxed. Go to your buttocks and feel them snuggling into the hot sand. Feel the joy of relaxing. Go to your back and talk to it. As you continue breathing tell your back to relax.

Feel your shoulders relaxing. Feel the quietness of your body. Talk to your arms and tell them to be quiet. See your hands and fingers. Go to them one at a time and feel them sink into the sand. Feel your neck, feel it relaxing. Go to your head and tell your forehead to relax. Think of your eyebrows and tell them to relax. Tell your eyes to be calm. Tell your cheeks to be quiet and calm. Feel your chin relaxing. Feel your ears being quiet and calm. Tell your hair and scalp to be calm. Your whole body is really warm and sinking into the sand. Quietly breathe in and out. Smell the ocean water. Hear the waves. Stay in this position and know you are in a quiet place. Your body feels soft and warm. See the palm trees around you swaying in the warm summer breeze. Let your consciousness quicken with this unfolding of your potential, as if you were in a time-lapse photograph.

Relax and know you are right in the moment. Feel the pure love of your higher spirit showering you in golden shafts of light coming down from the heavens. Feel its strength. In this state of pure bliss is the expression of pure self love joining and swirling with the light and love from above. In this calmness, you feel the pure love. This love radiates from you in light. It connects with the oneness of all wherever it falls. Take the time to enjoy the moment.

After a while, gently start to move and slowly stretch your body and open your eyes. Allow your mind and body to return to the present time and place. Be aware of how you feel. Take time to think about where you have been and enjoy this moment.

Do a Meditation

To meditate is to allow one to focus one's thoughts, to plan or project the mind. Doing regular meditation helps you to become more centered and balanced. This practice can create a less stressful life and assist you in your lessons. Unhealthy stress can cause a weakness of the immune system, which can allow illness to invade the body.

Do a mediation.

After the meditation: How do you feel?

Do you think meditation can assist you? If so how?

How often do you think you need to meditate?

Visualizations

𝒱isualization is the formation of mental visual images, the act or process of interpreting in visual terms, or of putting into visible form. The process of making a viscus visible by the introduction.

There are many ways we can think. We normally use logical thought. There are times when we introduce a new understanding of the solution to a situation. When this occurs, this thought is called intuition. This is when we begin to be in our creative mind. We use intuition to create new beginnings. This is where your new world begins.

A part of this process is called mental imagery. When we use the language of imagery, we are simply turning our thoughts into a mental picture. When we use this type of imaging, we connect it to our intention. For instance, if you wanted to build a house, you begin by setting forth your intention. You intend to build a house. You see the ground it is to be built on. You design the structure and choose the materials. The rooms start to develop. The colors are selected. It goes on to completion. You have planned with intention and guided your mind to the desired results. Then you set out to achieve the house. Now you will start to develop a plan to pay for it. That is when we must get really creative! If the intention and desire is there, you will accomplish the mission.

We can also use this imagery and visualization process to assist our healing. We always define our intention. What do you want to achieve? For example, if you have a headache your intention is to have it go away. You are giving yourself an inner instruction. It is like a computer program for your mind. It focuses on what you are working on. You tell yourself what you want to accomplish and be very clear about it. When your headache goes away, your confidence and success in using imagery will become more keen.

Intention depends on will and the choices we make. We give ourselves the direction and we find new paths to assist our lives. You have the right to contribute to your own healing.

Get into a state of healing with your mind the next time you have an illness of any kind.

Try this exercise:

Close your eyes. Do a simple meditation. (I am healthy.) Take a few minutes to get centered. (Talking to your Higher Power, asking to be connected to the universe or whatever you choose to do.) Tell yourself to be calm and quiet. (Talk to your body.) See yourself as clean inside and out. State your intention. (Such as to be healthy and clear.) Take a few deep breaths to relax. See your eyes becoming clear and very bright. Turn to the inside of your body. Imagine a white light at the top of your head. See this white light going down your body along your spine. Imagine the currents of this electrical system clearing out and cleansing each body system and organ. See it come down the head into the throat, down the chest, right down the spine. See it clearing all the limbs, clearing out all negativity in the blood and cells of your body. Take the light into the lowest part of your back, to the area of the fifth lumbar. Push that light into the earth. Push all the black strands of negativity into the earth. Fill up your body with the white light. See all the systems becoming pink and healthy. When both the rhythmic and light is filling up all the cavities, wrap yourself completely in white light. After some time, become aware of your breath. Let it come in and out. Slowly open your eyes. Take your time to return back to yourself. Listen to yourself, see how you feel. Your body will listen and respond.

When you have recovered from illness, some would say that this is just a coincidence. How could mental pictures have any effect on the elements of health? Our bodies are made up of energy. When you begin to work with this internal electrical system, you will find self-healing. There are many ways to work with your body. You have an inner knowledge of what your needs are. Just tune in to it and listen. You will be guided. It will become easier to stay focused as you continue the work of visualization. External quieting helps us to concentrate on going inward. Try to avoid everyday noises.

Cleansing is important in opening yourself up to becoming whole. It is an inner way of unburdening. When we bathe or shower, we experience a cleansing. For each of us, there is a moral indiscretion registered in our bodies. This can adversely influence the workings of our physical bodies. Our human desire is to remain in goodness. Remember, however, we are human. This is a part of our lesson. To heal ourselves, we must begin by cleaning up our act. It is a part of the conscious act. There is a part of us that remains in denial. We can use images and visualization to clear that path and allow a more healthy pattern to emerge.

Do a Visualization now on intention

Visualization is the formation of mental visual images. The act or process of interpreting in visual terms or of putting them into visual form. The process of making a viscus visible by introduction. There are many ways we can think. We normally use logical thought. There are times when we introduce a new understanding of a solution to a situation. When this occurs, this thought is called intuition. This is when we begin to be in our creative mind. We use this intuition to create our new beginnings.

Let's begin to turn our thoughts into a mental picture. Visualize in your mind a picture of something you want. It could be a new relationship, a change in your behavior, a better attitude, getting a new pet, the solution to a problem, or anything you want to have or change.

Remember, we cannot change another person, only ourselves. You begin by setting up your intentions. What do you want? What is your desire? Define your intention.

Give yourself an inner instruction. Be very clear about your intention. Intuition is your guide. If what you are doing is not correct, your intuition informs you. Follow that feeling.

Do a visualization.

What does this do for you?

What can be accomplished with the visualization?

What changes do you want in your journey?

How do you visualize a perfect life?

Are you satisfied?

Visualization

Creating a job

Write down a positive job you would like to have. Design it as the most perfect setting. Is it in an office or outside? See the job duties. Do you own this business? Where is the location? Find the type of people you want to work with. What kind of money will it provide? What are the hours? Who will you be working with? Why will it make you happy? What is in it for you? Write down the job you desire now.

Visualization

Creating a social life

Visualize a social life. What do you want to do? Who do you want in your life? Are you satisfied? Do you want more? Where do you start? Do you want to dance? Do you want to bowl? Do you want to do volunteer work? What about traveling? Perhaps a cruise? Are you interested in joining a group like a sorority or fraternity? What about a class? What are your interests? Classes are offered in so many areas. There are cooking classes, cards, painting, piano, languages, etc. The list is endless. What is your passion? What is interesting to you? Joining with your fellow persons gets you out among people and starts to enhance your life. Bring into yourself your dreams. This is your creation. What is exciting to you? Have it your way. Start a creation now. There are **NO LIMITS**. Write one down now.

Visualization of living place

Design a place you would like to live. Where is the location? What state? What town? What kind of house is it? Is it an apartment, condo, or private residence? Is it brick, wood, or stone? Does it have a garage? Is there a basement? Does it have more than one level? Go ahead, design the rooms. What are the colors in the house? Set up the furniture in the rooms. See the yard. Start writing a vision now.

Goals and Journals

Many people find it easier to keep their life on track if they set goals. Goals should be attainable, challenging, and realistic. Be sure what you set is what you can reach. People set goals by the week, month, or year. Begin by making a list, which includes the results you desire. Start with the most important ones. For instance, if you want to have $1000 saved by the end of the year, write down that goal. Figure out how much you can save by the day, week, or month. How much can you afford to put back? Will you put the money in a can or bank? Is this a reasonable amount? It this attainable and realistic? Write your goals down. Follow up on them on a regular basis. If you get off track one time, do not despair. Just begin again. Be proud of what you accomplish.

Journals provide an ideal tool for tracking plans, writing down what has happened with your goals and daily life. It is a way of tracking important records and events of your life. It can contain thoughts or feelings that come up during the day, personal or business activities, food you eat, and exercise. Personal and business expenses, financial investment data, health progress, weather or news of the day can be recorded. The possibilities are unlimited. It is an easy way to check future plans or refer back to your earlier years' entries. It can help you keep on track of your goals, affirmations, and progress. It could include a list of birthdays and anniversaries for the upcoming year. A person may discover many convenient and rewarding ways to use the journal. Journals provide a good tracking device to complete goals, activities, and progress that a person has achieved each year. Most people find journals work best with daily entries. Simply buy a notebook and begin writing entries. There are journals that can be purchased that have been set up to guide you in your entries. It does not matter what you write in them. Just begin. This is another way to help you in creating your life journey. Writing in your journal with gratitude will always give you positive results. What do you have to lose? Go ahead, try it and see if it enhances your life.

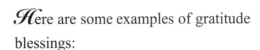

*H*ere are some examples of gratitude blessings:

Serenity in your life.	You saw a concert.
You watched a sunset.	You have good health.
You saw the mountains.	You saw the ocean.
A lovely day in your life.	You read a book
You were with loved ones.	You laughed.
You made a new friend.	You found a new job.
You received flowers.	You washed your car.
You spent the day fishing.	You had a new adventure.

You were able to pay your bills.
You visited your Grandparents.
You went to a movie with a friend.
You had a day of vacation to do nothing.
You see all the miracles in your life.

When you say Thank You, your higher power hears you and you feel like Heaven on Earth.

CONNECTION WITH UNIVERSAL SPIRITS

Along with the steps previously described, the following are other prayerful ways to strengthen us on our way, and are also important in achieving the fulfillment of our life's purpose. These are, Giving, Working in Silence, Giving out Blessings, Practicing Protection, and Universal Blessings.

Giving

*W*hat you give is what you get. This has been proven so many times. When we give of ourselves and give of our money, it truly returns in many ways. There are times when we have a choice, give our material things away or sell them. We may be short of money at times, yet we still give money away. When you see someone who needs what you have and you give it to them, it comes back to you so many times. Think of the times when someone gave to you.

The rewards are numerous. One day I was shopping and I found a small inexpensive radio to buy. There was a young girl around eight years of age standing by, who also wanted a radio. I asked where her mother was and she replied she was with her grandma. She told me her grandma didn't have money to buy the radio for her. I asked the grandmother if I could get it for her. She said, "no." I finally convinced her it was okay. I told the girl there was one stipulation to this deal. When she got to be a big girl and had a job, it would be necessary for her to buy a radio for another little girl. She promised to do that. It felt really nice to give her the gift, but, in some ways, it felt like it would mean more to her by giving her a goal of providing for another girl. I believe she will do it. It is called passing it on.

 **Giving exercise**

What can you do to increase your giving?

What changes do you have in mind?

Who will be your recipient?

How will you benefit?

Working in Silence

𝒯here are times when we do things for people silently. You find that when you do good things for someone, without their knowledge, it seems to be more beneficial in your own behalf. There is an understanding that good deeds are slated when they are given. When this deed has been told to another person or revealed in any way, the deed is not as worthy. It isn't that it didn't go down on the slate, it just wasn't given the same power as the silent ones. When you give money, gifts, or do good deeds when no one else knows, it becomes more special for yourself.

Give out Blessings

*L*et's begin by using a simple gesture. When you are out and about, or anytime you are among people, start offering *silent* verbal blessings. It is so easy when someone approaches you to *silently* offer "Have a nice healthy day" or "Blessings to you. " The more you do these things the better your days become. If you work in an office, take a moment to look around you and give a *silent* greeting to those around you.

Driving down the street, in a grocery store, it doesn't matter where you are at any time. Look for an opportunity to do something good that no one knows about. Each day, remember to give a *silent* gift. Let someone go before you in line. Help someone in some way. Go visit someone. Make a telephone call to someone for no particular reason, except to wish them a better day. Go to the hospital and have a visit with a patient there. Send a card to someone. Give of yourself in some manner. There are unlimited opportunities. When you do these things, all at once people start treating you in a different way. They are not aware of the subtle changes, but you will certainly notice. Remember what you offer is what you get. It has a rebounding effect. What do you want in your day? Give it away, so that you may have it.

Protection for yourself and others

Sometimes we feel uneasy about going on a drive or trip. You can connect to the universe and visualize a white light or cloud of light coming down from the heavens and circling your vehicle. Use this as a protection. Use this visualization to cover and protect your friends, family, or anything you want to protect. I used to do this every morning to many people, family, vehicles, houses, etc. I asked the universe to continue to protect them forever after I put forth the vision.

Special Universal Blessings

At 10:10pm every night, I ask the universe to provide special blessings to certain people. I constructed a list of those I want remembered. It's like building an address list on your computer or in your address book. It can contain as many people as you want. You can constantly add to this list. It is a prayerful way of extending yourself to their soul. It seems to be especially helpful to those who are hurting. It makes you feel good to know you are helping them. When a person appears to be in pain, and it feels like it would be helpful for them, I inform them they are a part of my list. This is especially true when someone asks me to pray for them.

For the most part, people do not know they are on this list. It seems to feel good to add those whose spirits have died. We ask our angel realm to send white light to those included on the list. We ask them to assist the person to their highest blessings. Pick a time. It helps you to commit to doing this. If you have someone who is always late to an appointment, tell them it is at 8:10 rather than straight up 8:00 and they are more likely to remember. Try to remember each day at whatever time you choose, to give it a thought and know it will be done. If you forget, don't worry because the universe is aware of your intention. You will find yourself feeling content or you may get warm feelings because you feel great about helping others. I have several people who are, or have been, ill on my list. Some have been told they are on this list. They told me they felt a presence and knew they were being assisted. Some people who have this training said they have seen and felt many changes in their life, health, and feelings.

Universal Blessings

Who do you want the universe to bless?

What time will you assign?

Write out your intention.

Start building your list now. Write it out.

Magical Solutions

𝒯he information given in this book is designed to help you achieve a happier, healthier life on a day to day basis. While it is spiritual in nature, it is also practical, "down to earth" in purpose. The following are some of the everyday applications I have discovered in living this lifestyle. It works like magic to solve situations.

Get your parking place

*O*ne of the easy methods that many of you have used that confirm this belief is a simple exercise.

When you are driving down the street or looking for a parking place in a parking lot, simply state "I need a parking spot right now. " Say this out loud or quietly to yourself. For instance, if it's raining, you may need a space close to the store where you plan to shop. It's always amazing how someone will pull out and a spot will become available to you. My son informed me he didn't need this exercise because he preferred to park way out so no one would bang up his car. Sometimes you just can't get ahead of your children. For the rest of us, this works.

Finding lost articles

When you have lost something or misplaced it there is a way to assist yourself in achieving its return. Place yourself in a quiet space mentally. Visualize a circle around your body. This circle can be a light from the heavens or universe. See the lost article or item in a hand. See the hand coming into your circle to claim the article. Think, "this is mine and I need it right now. " The more you do this, the quicker it seems to appear. If it does not appear suddenly, do not despair. Continue doing the meditation and the article will come back.

One person I know did this meditation. The last thing her husband had given her before he died was a piece of jewelry. The jewelry disappeared. She used this meditation for a year. In the meantime, she had moved to a different residence. She assumed the article was lost during the move. She continued to do the meditation. Over a year later she opened a drawer and there was the piece she had lost.

Our house was burglarized several years ago. One of my children, Shane, lost among other things, some of his jewelry, including a cross his grandmother had given him, several chains, and a special ring. I told him to ask for it back. Several months went by. One day when I arrived home from work, his father told me he was mowing the grass and he saw something shining in the grass. He stopped the mower to look. He found a trail of the lost jewelry. It went from the ditch to the house. Everything was returned. It certainly made a believer out of Shane.

One day I was cooking dinner when my granddaughter, Amber, told me grandpa had lost his car keys. I said, "he needs to ask for them. " My daughter-in-law, Dawn, said "if you are so good why don't you find them?" I said, " I would but I am busy. " Later, I decided it would be best to take the time, so I asked the universe, " where are the keys?" I went into the garage and looked in the car at the ignition. They were not there. I walked over to a tool cabinet. There was a cloth over the top of the tool cabinet. I removed the cloth and found the keys. I took them into the house and gave them to him. Amber said, "Grandpa said you hid his keys. " Oh well!

My son Shane was always losing things. I was constantly reminding him rather than panic and go running around the house looking, to take a moment to stop and do this easy mediation. It makes life so much calmer. I hope he is doing this.

It seems like everyone loses the keys to their house or car. When this happens ask for them.

Have you ever noticed how little kids can find things we lose? Could it be they know to just ask for them? When your family asks you for lost articles, what is the first thing you do? Do you say, "where did you put them?" This is one method of asking the universe to assist us.

Stop and take the time to try this and save yourself some time and energy.

Finding lost articles

What have you lost?

Ask for the lost article now. Use the light meditation.

Never give up. You know if at first you do not succeed, try again over and over.

Creating your Council

We can create a council to assist us. It works well to find a set of angels or spirits of your choice to sit on this board. We can visualize it.

See a board room. A room with a table and chairs. Start placing your council in the positions or chairs. For instance, you may want Jesus as the head of your council. Perhaps you have a relative or close friend who has died and is on the other side and you want to include their spirit. My grandmother was very special and close to me. She and my father are among those on my board. I feel very close to some of my family that has gone on, and there is still a bond, so it is comforting for me to include them. I also have special angels who sit on my board. This is a place where you can go for answers to some of life's dilemmas. This board has the answers to your problems.

You visualize the room and those you allow into the room. Put forth your intentions when you build them. What do you expect? What do you need from this Council? Give this council your situation and watch for answers. They may come as whispers in your thoughts. Answers may come to you in a vision. The answer may come in conversations with another person. It's not that the counsel doesn't know your problems. They just need your agreement to give you assistance. Know they are always available and ready to help you. When you put forth your thought, they go to work. They do not intervene until asked for their help. The answers will always be in your higher interest. Trust your intuition, the answer is correct.

A friend of mine was buying a house and got into some problems. She called me to ask for help. She was very frustrated. I helped her build her council. She said she had trouble connecting with them at first. She felt they just stared at her. She finally started asking questions. At that time, the energy changed. She began to receive her answers. The deal on the house went very smoothly. It worked out beautifully.

There are people who will tell me they don't need this. They pray only to God. That is fine. They should continue on that path. For the rest of us, God has sent messengers to assist us. We all want what is best for ourselves.

Creating a Council

Write it down. Set up a council, imagine the setting and place.

What is the intention?

How will you use this council?

Who are the board members?

Creating your new position in life

If you are wanting a new position in your job or a change in your life, create it. Get into a meditative state and begin to visualize it. If it's a new job, design it in your mind. Pick out the position. Select the type of company you want to work at. See the room you will be working in. Pick out the carpet and equipment. Select the people you will work with. See their energy as matching yours. See yourself being offered the job and accepting it. See contracts being signed or whatever the need is to get the position. Imagine the paycheck being given to you, see the amount as what you need. Ask the Angels and Universe to help you.

If you want to move to a new city, see that city. Imagine where it is. Find the location. See the environment. See yourself loading the car or getting on the airplane. Imagine it step by step as it happens.

If you want a new apartment or home, put a plan in your mind. Focus on the how many rooms there will be. Set them up as you want them. Is it a two story? Does it have a basement? Is it in the country or city? Is it near water? Will it include other people living with you? Where will they sleep? What is the design of this house? Does it have a single garage? Include everything you can think of.

If you are in a management position and you are not getting the results you would like, put it into your focus. See the staff working. Go to their higher selves and ask or tell them what you need from them. You can visualize a room full of your workers and see them at the conference table. Put a white light around the room and see light on each of them. Visualize them as happy and productive individuals. Ask them to provide what it will take to get the job done. If it is a result oriented position, see a board on the wall and visualize it showing the results you want. Tell the people how proud of them you are and THANK them.

Once you start this process there are no limits to what will happen in your world. THERE ARE NO LIMITS. Get creative. Come up with a plan to move forward. This is your world. Create it the way you want it. Have fun.

Working with Illness

𝒯he first thing to remember is we create what we get and it's all to experience our lessons. If you become ill, know at some level you need this experience. When it's over, you will be better for it. How can we enjoy good health if we never saw the other side of it? Let's say you have a headache. You can keep acknowledging it and continue with the pain. Or you can start doing a meditation. When you get in a healthy space, do some visualizations.

There are many ways to do this. Start being aware of your breath. Keep breathing at an even pace. Feel it coming in and out. Do this for a few minutes. Get relaxed and begin to talk to your body. Tell it to be quiet. Start with your toes and work up to your head. Do not leave any system out. After you have quieted your body, start to see a white light coming into the crown of your head. See this light go all the way to the end of your spine. See the light go into the floor or ground. See it go all the way into the earth.

It goes clear into the center of the earth. Tell your body to send the negative energy down this stream of light into the earth, and the earth will convert it into fresh new clean energy. You can add to this visualization by seeing all your systems as clean, pink, happy, and working together.

You can use this with any problem you are having. It is helpful to affirm, "I am healthy. " Remember the more you tell the universe and yourself that you are healthy, the more it becomes the reality. There is no such thing as terminal. Yes, we are all going to return to the source at some time. You are in control and working with the universe until that time.

Working with your higher power

Sometimes we get into a situation and need to be able to reach a person in a different way. For instance, you might want to give some information to someone you are having difficulty reaching. Perhaps you are not getting along with this person. You want to tell them the way the two of you are interacting is hurtful to you. You need to give them a message and you think they may not accept this information. This is a way to reach them, and they will not be able to refuse. Always use this for a positive reason. Never misuse this opportunity.

You call in your higher self and Guardian Angel, and ask the person for their higher self and their Guardian Angel to join you. Take them to a mountain top and see benches at the top facing each other. Visualize them and begin to explain what you want them to hear. They can't refuse to attend. Give yourself plenty of time to explain what you want them to know. After you talk to them, you thank them for listening and come back to reality. Know that the information was taken in by their conscience and, at a different level they heard you. They will process this and come to a conclusion of what has been said to them and how it affects them. Usually they will come forward in some manner and you will see positive results.

One time I was playing with this situation when I asked a fellow to dance with me at a party. He politely refused, giving no reason, just refused. When I got home, I was thinking about how it hurt my feelings. The ego steps forward. I decided to try this method of reaching him. I did the mountain vision and went to a party a week or so later. It was amusing how it worked. The man came walking by and seemed startled and stopped in front of me. He turned to me and said, "I owe you a dance. " I said, "Yes, you do. " He said, "I will come back and dance with you later," and he did. It was like an experiment to see if it worked. There have been times when I would feel something in a relationship was not going well and if I took the time to do these things, it always turned out better.

There are many ways to create such a scene. Use

your imagination and find a stream, river, or whatever feels good to you. We can create many different environments. The main thing is to better ourselves and those with whom we choose to work.

Working with others

𝓘f you are working with a person and there appears to be some discomfort, perhaps you are having a constant difference of opinion. Take a mirror with eight sides and put it on a wall between you with the mirror side facing them. Tape it under a picture or place it under a object or behind a file. You are sending their negative energy back to them.

When you are dealing with a person who is being verbally abusive to you and they are in the process of giving you their opinion, discussing their views in a loud voice, they are usually things you have heard before. The person giving the information is usually suffering because of their own problems. It may not even be the situation at hand. He or she is usually out of control, angry, or it may be fear. The thing you can do is visualize bubbles. Remember when you were a child and you had the bubble holder and created the bubbles? Recapture that moment see the bubbles as pink, floating around the room.

Send the person bubbles full of love and good energy. In other words, remove yourself from the disorder. It serves no purpose to listen to the discord. When they are finished stating their opinion, you can return to the room. There will be feelings of serenity on your part. It makes it much easier to deal with the situation.

Cleaning out your space

In order to do our best work, we need to keep our energy and thoughts as clean as possible. Try to create an attitude of positive energy. Try to stop being judgmental. Try to understand others are learning their lessons too. Give one "positive" away every day. Let someone have their way, even if it's as small as letting a person in front of you in line or calling a friend to say "hello." Be aware of conscious giving. Give up fear. The biggest fear is fear itself. Try to let the ego go. You are a wonderful, kind person. Love yourself. You don't need to have the ego in the way. When thoughts of your being higher or better than another person in any way presents itself, face it, and tell it to stop. In the whole process, you will be better. Life will proceed in a kinder manner.

Clean out your head. Start a meditation, and when you are calm, look into the void. To do this is like seeing nothing, just a quiet space with no outside interference. Imagine there is a room in your head. It's right in the middle. Think about your head having a line on the forehead to back of your head and a line ear to ear. In the center of these lines is where you find this room. Check its size and see what is in there. Clean it out. If you see furniture, get it out. If you see people, have them leave. No matter what you see, have it clear and clean. Every once in a while during meditation, check this room. We need it clean and white with light from the universe. We do our best work with our own house clean.

Keep thinking kind thoughts. See happy and contentment in your space. May your life lessons be easy.

The Blessing

My rose, my gift to you: Find time to enjoy each precious moment. Find the love for yourself and your fellow persons you have joined here on earth. May your life lessons be easy. Connect with the Universe, our God, your higher Self, your Angels. Acknowledge your path. This is *your* life and *your* lesson. Find the fulfillment of your dreams. My wish for you is to have Balance, Harmony and most of all Peace in your Journey of Life. You deserve the best. *Create* it.

Blessings
Patricia

Glossary

Affirmation
Affirming a positive statement

Akashic Records
Akashic is a Sanskrit word meaning primary substance. It is like a computer containing all the information of the soul's travel since its beginning. It tracks every thought, word, and deed of one's soul's lifetime. Sometimes it is referred to as the Universal Mind. It contains all events, occurrences and knowledge.

Angels
A spiritual being superior to man in power and intelligence. They come as Guardian Angels to guide us with influences and may intervene to protect us from harm. There is a hierarchy within the angel realms. The levels of power are Angels, Archangels, Principalities, Powers, Virtues, Dominions, Thrones, Cherubim and Seraphim.

Chakras

Chakras are energy vortices. They could be described as rotating wheels and they spin like a top. There are seven main chakras, they are aligning the spiritual body and vibrate at the frequency of the seven colors of the rainbow which combines to create white light.

Conscious

The sense of consciousness of the moral goodness of one's own intentions. A power or principle enjoining good acts. The part of the super ego in psychoanalysis that transmits command and admonition to the ego.

Consciousness

Share of knowledge or awareness of an inward act. State of emotion and thought.

Dimension

A plane of existence. A position in space.

Dimensions

First dimension: Lowest form or vibration; sometimes called the mineral kingdom.

Second dimension: Known as the plant kingdom. Life exists as patterns in nature.

Third dimension: The human and animal kingdom.

Fourth dimension: Relates to time and space. It is sometimes referred to as the transition between the physical world and the higher worlds of the Celestials. It has been portrayed as the vibration that begins to open the heart and a portal, providing a pathway to higher worlds.

Fifth Dimension: It is where we go, after we have been transformed into a higher form of God consciousness. Celestial beings reside here.

Sixth Dimension: It is known as the bridge between lower worlds and higher creations.

Seventh Dimension: It is where the Universal laws and Ascended Masters reside. It has been referred to as the seventh heaven.

Ego

The one of the three divisions of the psyche in psychoanalytic theory that serves as the organized conscious mediator between the person and reality by functioning both in perception of and adaptation to reality. The ego can cause one to be self-centered and selfish because it limits one's outlook.

Energy Field

The electromagnetic energy that is around a being.

Energy Blocks

This is a perception of reality that will cause us to become out of balance and harmony with the universe.

Goal

The end toward which effort is directed.

Higher self

It is an extension of self that is filled with light and contains the God Force.

Intuition

The ability to connect with our higher selves. Listen for the inner voice

Journal
A service book containing entries of information.

Kharma
Kharma is the basic principles of individual existence conforming to divine law. It defines the destiny of each soul. This is the result of all our thoughts, words, and deeds. All karma is documented in our Akashic records.

Kundalini
Kundalini is located at the base of your spine. This area of your spine is sometimes referred to as the center of gravity. Kundalini is a source of power and liquid energy. This power can release itself. Most people who experience this are those who engage in meditation. If it releases itself, you have different sensations as it works its way through the chakras. You may feel a buzzing sensation, become light headed and experience other feelings. It is referred to as a Kundalini rush. This power can move one into a higher dimension of spiritual growth.

Masters

Those who have evolved spiritually and assist in ruling the world.

Meditate

Meditation is to allow one to focus one's thought or to plan or project the mind. It is a way of centering your soul.

Soul

The immaterial essence, animating principle or actuating cause of an individual life. The spiritual principle embodied in human beings. The soul has the function of thinking and determining behavior.

Spirit

The immaterial intelligent or sentient part of a person.

Unconsciousness

Upper level of mental thought. A person is aware with unconsciousness process.

Visualization

Visualization is a formation of mental visual images, the act or process of interpreting in visual terms, or of putting it into visible form.

Vortex

A magnetic grid system. They are an energy that is spiritual and magnetic in nature. If you are sensitive toward them, you can feel them upon entering the areas in which they exist.

NOTES

NOTES

NOTES